Are You Sitting Comfortably?

Brian Moses lives on the Sussex coast with his wife and two daughters. He writes and edits poetry for young people. He travels extensively both in the UK and abroad presenting his poetry and percussion shows in schools and libraries. When he isn't travelling he is always being told off by his family for sitting too comfortably when he should be mowing the lawn or cleaning out the guinea pigs.

Jane Eccles has been an illustrator for many years. Her favourite things are her family, her cat Wilfrid, the seaside in Dorset, watching *ER* and eating vast amounts of chocolate.

Are You Sitting Comfortably?

Story poems
chosen by Brian Moses

Illustrated by Jane Eccles

MACMILLAN CHILDREN'S BOOKS

*For children and staff at the Elementary Department of
Frankfurt International School and particularly for
Sharon Morgenstern and her love of literature*

First published 2002
by Macmillan Children's Books
a division of Macmillan Publishers Ltd
20 New Wharf Road, London N1 9RR
Basingstoke and Oxford
www.panmacmillan.com
Associated companies throughout the world

ISBN 0 330 39704 4

A CIP catalogue record for this book is available from the British Library.
Printed by Mackays of Chatham plc, Chatham, Kent.

Contents

A Visit to Yalding – John Coldwell 1

Break Out at Arkwright's Shop – David Harmer 6

Alexander – Dave Calder 8

Beauty Sleep – Celia Warren 10

The Sleeping Ugly – Marian Swinger 12

Cindy Reller – Clare Bevan 15

Red Squirrels – Daphne Kitching 18

The Tomcat of Notre Dame – Adrian Henri 20

Techno-Child – Adrian Mitchell 24

Letters to the Three Pigs – Clare Bevan 26

A Ghostly Tale – Roger Stevens 28

The Witch and the AA Man – Barry Buckingham 35

The River's Story – Brian Patten 38

Late Home – Brian Lee 40

Everything's Fine – John Foster 44

Death of a Ghost – Gareth Owen 46

The Cupboard on the Landing – John Coldwell 52

The Curse of Cortachy – Patricia Leighton 54

Cows on the Beach – Matthew Sweeney 56

Danielle's Dragon – Brian Moses   58

The Election – Valerie Bloom   60

Parentade – Philip Waddell   64

A Tall Story – John Mole   68

Spinning a Good Yarn – Read On – Patricia Leighton 70

Not History, Her Story – Moira Andrew   72

Puss-in-footie-boots – James Carter   74

Hansel – Mick Gower   77

Haunted Dunwich (a true story) – Marian Swinger   80

The Weekend Camp – Brian Moses and Ian Souter   81

A True Story – David Harmer   92

The Path to Lee – Clare Bevan   94

A Go'st Story! – Ray Mather   96

Girl Power – Les Baynton   97

A Visit to Yalding

We went to Yalding to look at the locks
To watch the water going up and down.
My brother found a dead sparrow to take home,
My mum found a ten pence piece,
My dad picked up a tin can that an animal might hurt
    itself on
And I –
I fell in the river.

I dripped back to the car.
'You're not getting into the car like that,'
said Dad. 'You'll ruin the upholstery.'
'You're not getting into the car like that,'
said Mum. 'You'll catch your death of cold.
Get those wet things off.'
I took off my squelchy shoes.
I took off my soggy socks.
And stopped.
'And the rest,' said Mum.
'No, Mum, please.'
'No one will see.'
'I can see,' said my brother.

'No looking.'
Off came the saturated shorts.
'I can see his pants.
I can see his pants.
And they're wet,' said my brother helpfully.

'They're not.'
'Get them off,' said Mum.
'No, Mum, please.'
'Don't be such a big drip.
Are you going to take them off
Or shall I?'
Down came the pants.
I sat on a towel in the car
next to my brother who was near wetting himself
    with laughter.
'What's it like to
What's it like to
What's it like to
have no pants?'

'Mum. Tell him.
Mum?
Dad?
Stop laughing.
It's not funny.'
'You're right,' said Dad.
There was a moment's silence
Then they all started laughing again.
Could my life ever reach a lower ebb?
It did at the end of our road.

'Oh. Isn't that Pamela Whitethorn?'
said my brother.
'Where?'
I looked.
It was.
'You love her.'
'I don't.'
'Do. Otherwise you wouldn't be blushing.'
'I'm not blushing.'
People always go red when they've fallen in the river
Everybody knows that.'
'Shall I tell her you haven't got any pants on?'
'You dare.'
'That's enough,' said Mum.

The shame.
Pantless before Pamela.

Through the window, I peeped at Pamela.
She was looking right at me.
Pamela knew things.
She knew where babies came from.
I wondered whether boys sitting in cars with no
    pants on
Looked any different to boys sitting in cars with
    pants on.
I waved in a casual 'I've got my pants on' sort of way.
If there was a difference
Pamela would know.

John Coldwell

Break Out at Arkwright's Shop

Break out said the budgies, *bust out* barked the dogs
Find freedom now called the tree creeping frogs.
Vamoose said the mice, the rats and the snakes
That's right said the cats, *we've got what it takes.*

The door slowly opened, Arkwright was back
he heard a slight squeak, he heard a faint crack
then he was showered with cages and hutches
as the pets flooded out escaping his clutches

When they got to the doorway they came to a stop
He cried out loud, *you all love this shop*
you need me too much, you can't run away
now hop back and pop back, and do it today!

They laughed at his words, looked under a shelf
Where a small cardboard box crawled along by itself,
You've got it all wrong, he heard a dog shout,
we're just making sure the tortoise gets out.

David Harmer

Alexander

King Alexander, third of Scotland,
really loved his wife a lot and
always tried to hurry home –
(This was long before the phone
was thought up by another Scot
called Alex, so the king could not
just call to say he'd been delayed
by work, bad weather or a plague.)

So, one night in 1286, the king
(who'd got stuck in a council meeting
in Edinburgh) got on his horse
and, with a few friends of course
for kings are never left alone,
set off to ride back to his home
to have his dinner with his wife
across the Firth of Forth in Fife.

A storm was rising. In the rain
they crossed the river. No train
was due for some six hundred years
so a boat took them (the ferry piers
are still there) and on the other shore
remounted and rode on once more –
travel in those days wasn't easy,
I'm sure that they were sore and queasy.

But Alex wouldn't hesitate:
he'd been king since he was eight,
survived rebellions and plots,
defeated invaders and got
back the Western Isles – he was not
going to let bad weather stop
him getting home in time for tea.
So on he galloped, recklessly.

It's not so far to Aberdour,
perhaps it took them half an hour,
but after that the darkness fell
And soon none of the men could tell
where they were. But the horses knew
and so they stumbled on. Just a few
miles before the castle at Kinghorn,
his queen, his dinner, a warm
fire and dry clothes, the king's good luck
ran out. In the dark fate struck.

His horse went the wrong way, and with
him on it, tumbled off a cliff.

Both dead. And in that moment history
changed completely. That one wrong turn
led to war, to Wallace, Bannockburn,
the Bruce, the Stewarts, all that came to be.

And Alexander never got his tea.

Dave Calder

Beauty Sleep

I've had a horrible hundred years;
I tossed and turned for twenty.
I thought I'd never get off to sleep
And, nightmares! – I've had plenty.

Halfway through the third decade
My eyes began to close,
Then just for six or seven years
I enjoyed a gentle doze

Till I woke up all of a sudden:
It was one of those lumpy beds,
Where springs dig into your ribcage
And stop you grabbing your zeds.

I turned the pillow over.
I needed my beauty sleep,
But I only managed a two-year kip;
Nothing nice and deep.

My finger kept on throbbing,
I know I shouldn't carp,
But all century it nagged me,
That spindle was so sharp.

Then just after ninety-nine years
When, at last, I'd started to snooze,
A prince came telling me, 'Wake up, please!'
How ever could I refuse?

I suppose he is quite handsome
And was simply doing his duty
So I only gave him one black eye
When he woke his Sleeping Beauty.

Celia Warren

The Sleeping Ugly

She was the Sleeping Beauty's
less famous cousin
and at her christening,
her mum and dad
managed to offend
no less than three fairies.
As a result
they had to call her Ugly.
Otherwise she got the same
curse as her cousin.
The Sleeping Beauty's dad
ordered all spindles
out of the kingdom.
The Sleeping Ugly's dad
bought a job lot and scattered
them about the castle.
After all, it's almost impossible
to interest a prince
in an ugly princess.
Well, the Sleeping Beauty
pricked her finger
when she was sixteen
in spite of all the precautions.
The Sleeping Ugly's dad
gave her a spindle
for her sixteenth birthday.
At the end of a hundred years,
a handsome prince kissed
the Sleeping Beauty

and they lived happily ever after.
A few princes had a look
at the Sleeping Ugly
then went back to their castles
without bothering.
So there she lay,
covered in cobwebs.
A hundred more years passed.
Then another
Then some more.
In the year 2000
the council decided to
build a new shopping centre
on the site of the old castle.
There wasn't much left
of it after all.
Just a dungeon
and a few stones.
They'd put the Sleeping Ugly
down there a few centuries back
to make room for an en suite.
A demolition man
who just so happened
to be an ex-prince
of Ruritania found her.
He hacked away the cobwebs
and revealed the body,
all six feet three of it
and a size eight to boot.
He was overcome by her beauty.
After all, standards of beauty change
in eight hundred years.

As a prince, even an ex-prince,
he knew what to do.
After he had kissed her,
the Sleeping Ugly's eyes opened.
'About time too,' she said.
They were married
the following day
after she had changed her name
to Naomi Moss.
Now she's a top model,
and the ex-prince is her manager.
Her picture is in
all the best magazines.
Paparazzi chase them
wherever they go
and they are seen
at all the celebrity hot spots.
They lived happily ever
after, of course.

Marian Swinger

Cindy Reller

Cindy Reller
Read the News,
'Royal Disco,
Rock & Blues.'
Knew her clothes were
Far too scruffy,
(Cleaning jobs don't
Pay enuffy.)

Boris Buttons
(Kind but poor)
Helped her brush the
Café floor.
'Cheer up, Cindy,
There's a chance
You may still go
To the dance.
My last pound could
Set you free
If you try the
Lottery.'

On the TV
Screen that night
Cindy's numbers
Sparkled bright.
Up she jumped from
Battered chair,
'I've become a
Millionaire!'
Sold her story
To the press,
Bought a cool
Designer dress,
Crossed the town to
Meet her Prince
Wearing shoes that
Made her wince . . .

. . . Kicked the shiny
Things away,
Danced barefoot till
Break of day,
While the Prince
Turned up his nose
At the sight of
Cindy's toes,
Chose instead her
Ugly sister
(A girl prepared to
Risk a blister.)

Meanwhile Cindy
Didn't care –
Bought the Café
In the Square,
Changed its name to
'Dream Come True'

AND

MARRIED BUTTONS!
(Quite right too.)

Clare Bevan

Red Squirrels

They said they'd seen red squirrels, the people we passed
   on the way up.
It was steep and rough and my legs ached long before
   the climb was done.
The climb to see the waterfall.
Seventy feet of tumbling, roaring water.
It would be good to have a picture of me being brave
   near the edge.
But I'd *rather* see red squirrels.

We met more people who said they'd seen them, high up
   amongst the trees.
Not the common, greedy, grey invaders, but *red*
   squirrels.
We'd see for ourselves, they said.
But we didn't.
We reached the waterfall sticky and tired.
We stood and admired it for what seemed like hours.
At last we began the trek down through the woodland.
Surely we'd spot them this time.
Stumbling over roots, I scanned the trees.
But nothing – no movement, no glint of red fur.
We saw cases from beech nuts cracked open and empty,
Oak trees and pine trees galore.
We saw long, ash-black slugs and fat, jet-black beetles.
We videoed rare butterflies.
But *I* wanted to see red squirrels.

We were almost down to the easy path
When, there before us, on the ground, we saw him.
Camouflaged by crisp, brown leaves and fading bracken,
Confident and poised, he held the stage,
Then darted off – a flash of rusty brightness.
Small and beautiful, belonging to this woodland.
And we had seen him.
Like getting a six to start a board game, now we'd done
    it once, it was easy.
Three times we spotted him before he vanished.
Warm and flushed with success we reached the bottom,
Passing some people who were starting the climb.
'Have a good climb,' we encouraged,
'By the way – *we've* seen red squirrels . . .'

Daphne Kitching

The Tomcat of Notre Dame

High above the roofs of Paris
Lives the Tomcat of Notre Dame
Looking down at the passers-by
Ready to save them from harm

The River Seine below him
He watches the boats go by
All set to swing to the rescue
In a twinkling of an eye

Catching a baby pigeon
Or a puppy from under a bus
Saving a drowning kitten
Never making a fuss

The bells made him slightly deaf
But he'll never miss a call
Swinging down a bell-rope
Clambering down a wall

Amid the wheels and pulleys
And the thunderous sound of bells
Lonely amongst the gargoyles
He'll sometimes pull faces as well.

The lovely Esmerelda
Is the apple of his eye
Green-eyed, black and slinky
He sees her with a sigh

'She's the Belle of the Flower Market
The toast of Gay Paree
All the young toms serenade her
How *could* she love someone like me?

She should have a cosy home
With cream and a welcome mat
Not a corner of tower alone
With a poor Cathedral cat'

And then one summer evening
Perched on top of a spire
Listening to the organ
And the singing of the choir

He heard a sound from far below
A muffled miaow for help
He sprang from peak to pinnacle
Not caring if he fell

From a darkened doorway
There came a scuffling sound
Two rough cats were struggling
With a figure on the ground

Downwards on a rope he swung
Sending the villains flying
Through the dusk he swarmed back up
His trembling burden crying

Behind a flying buttress
He laid it on the floor
Two green eyes slowly opened
She gently took his paw

'My hero! If you want me
I'll stay and share your life
Up here above the rooftops
I'll be your loving wife.'

Now they're together paw-in-paw
She'll never come to harm
The lovely Esmerelda
And the Tomcat of Notre Dame

High above the roofs of Paris
Live the Tomcat and his Madame
As the sun sets over the River Seine
And the towers of Notre Dame.

Adrian Henri

Techno-Child

My dad was a kung fu fighter in a video game called
    Death Cult Army
He lurked around on the seventh level waiting for smug
    contestants so he could chop them up like salami
He was good for nothing but kick jab punch gouge
    headbutt kick in the bum
And all his friends were stuperollificated when he fell in
    love and married my mum

My mum was a thirty-two-colour hologram at a Medical
    Convention in Beverly Hills
She represented the Statue of Liberty and she advertised
    Anti-Indigestion Pills
She was half the size of the statue itself and the tourists
    she attracted were fewer
And if you ever reached out to touch her robes, well
    your hand just went straight through her.

They met in the Robocop Theme Park on a hullabaloo
    of a night
When my dad saw off some Gremlins on Camels who
    had challenged Mum to a fight
They sat together and watched the moon from a
    swing-chair on Popeye's porch
Then my father proposed in Japanese and my mother
    she dropped her torch.

They were married and put on a floppy disc by
    the Bishop of IBM
Pac-Man, Count Duckula and all the Power Rangers
    came and celebrated with them
The fun was going ballistic but it nearly ended
    in tears
For those old Space Invaders started a ruck with
    the Mortal Kombateers

Since my mum's a mirage of electrons and my dad
    is strictly 2-D
You may wonder how I was born at all in this
    Virtual Reality
Well they're close as a Mouse and its Mouse-mat
    and they taught me just what I should do –
I fight video-gamesters and indigestion with
    pills and a torch and kung fu.

Adrian Mitchell

Letters to the Three Pigs

(Found in a Gingerbread Filing Cabinet, at the 'King of the Castle' Planning Office.)

Dear Mr Pig, We notice
You've built a house of straw.
You didn't ask permission,
You didn't say what for,
You didn't ring our office,
You didn't write, and so –
Our Big Bad Wolf will be RIGHT ROUND
To huff and puff and blow.

Dear Pig & Co., We're puzzled.
Some creatures never learn.
You've built a house of wooden planks –
The sort that's bound to burn,
The sort that's full of woodworm,
The sort that causes trouble –
Our Big Bad Wolf will be RIGHT ROUND
To smash your place to rubble.

Pig Partners, Now you've done it.
You're either rude or lazy.
You've gone and built a house of bricks
To drive our planners crazy.
You didn't dig foundations,
You knew we'd have to ban it –
Our Big Bad Wolf will be RIGHT ROUND
To blast you off the planet.

Dear Brothers Pig, Our greetings!
We huffed, we puffed, we blew,
We even stormed your chimney,
But NOTHING bothered you –
Our Big Sad Wolf will be RIGHT ROUND
To pay you our respects,
And offer you a splendid job
With Beanstalk Architects.

Clare Bevan

A Ghostly Tale

It was a Wednesday, I recall
Around five o'clock.
October, getting dark
The Design and Technology Room quiet
Only the soft belch of ancient radiators
Disturbing the peace.
And the wind crying on the playground.

I was marking some cranes
Crazy contraptions of badly planed wood
Concoctions of wire and pulleys and string
When I heard a dog whining
As though hurt
As though abandoned

So I went outside
Looking for the dog
Looking for the owner
Nothing
Only dark shadows
And the wind playing kiss chase
With crisp packets.

I'd have thought no more of it
But exactly one week later,
Wednesday, five o'clock
Alone in my classroom,
There it was again.
Dog on the playground
Crying at the moon
A chilling sound.

There was the moon.
An early moon in a crisp star-studded sky
The old Victorian buildings
Silhouetted against the last smudgy streaks
Of sunset.
No dog.

But back in the classroom
I could still hear it.
A sad, lonesome sound.
It was coming from the storeroom.
Where I stored wood, perspex sheets
Years of accumulated junk.
I crept across the room
And listened at the door.
No mistake – there was the weird whining.
Gingerly I creaked open the door.

Slowly.
Easy now.
No dog sprang out –
Angry and annoyed
Or eager and tail-waggingly pleased.
But still the noise.
It was coming from the loft.

There was a trapdoor
In the storeroom ceiling
But I'd never opened it.
I listened to the whiny, snuffly
Doggy noise
Disturbing the school's sleeping ghosts
And heard another sound.
A tip-tapping sound.
The gentle tip-tapping
Of wood upon wood
Or maybe bone upon bone.
And so I did
What any other teacher would have done
In those circumstances.
I went home.

Over the next few months,
As autumn gave way to Christmas
And Christmas to the cold keen winds of
The naked New Year,
I heard the noises often.

Never when the room was full
Of the warm sounds
Of wood being worked
Of plans being discussed
Of hammer on nail or thumb
But when the room was silent
And I was on my own
Only then I'd hear the soft desperate whining
And the tip-tapping
Tip-tap
Tip-tap
Tip-tap

As Easter burst upon the stage
All was about to change
A new life for the school
A new life for me.
The school was leaving its dreary Victorian building,
Leaving its poky classrooms
Its dilapidated loos and old-fashioned desks
For a brand new building half a mile away.
I was leaving for a new school
Leaving my old workshop of disused lathes,
Abused benches and slow hand clamps

And so it came to pass
That on the last day of term
I helped Ken the caretaker
Carry the aluminium ladder
Through the sad, stripped classroom
To the bare storeroom
Ken pushed the ladder up to the trapdoor
And carefully climbed.
He looked at me for reassurance. I nodded.
He took a deep breath
And banged the trapdoor.

An explosion of muck and dust
Filled the confined space.
But in my mind I could only hear
The soft doggy whine
The tip-tap
Tip-tap
Darkness spilled out.
Ken crawled into the black hole, his torch held high.
I heard him gasp.

Soon we both stood in the loft
And gazed down
Hardly believing our eyes.
Lying between the joists
Curled in the dust of a century
Dull-white in the pale torch light
The skeleton of a dog
And in its jaws
Clenched for all eternity
A stick.

(I did indeed leave the school. The dog's skeleton was cleaned and is now an exhibit in the school's new science laboratory.)

Roger Stevens

The Witch and the AA Man

Old Peggotty Witch had a problem –
she had to reach Blackpond by eight.
The Witches' Convention would start then,
and nobody liked to be late.

Her broomstick refused to get going,
although it had made many flights.
She kicked at the twigs in frustration,
but that only laddered her tights.

The usual words to get airborne
she'd said twenty times,
maybe more.
But never a twitch did the broom make.
It stayed, looking dead, on the floor.

But then she remembered the AA,
and gave them a telephone call.
And soon a young fellow was standing,
with toolbox,
in Peggotty's hall.

He hadn't much knowledge of broomsticks,
so didn't know what to check first.
They don't have an engine or cables,
or things that can fracture or burst.

It didn't require any petrol.
No handbrake was holding it back.
And nothing new could be discovered
by raising it up on a jack.

But this was a thoughtful young fellow –
most helpful and enthusiastic.
A catapult start he suggested,
but that needed too much elastic.

Now Peggotty Witch had the sniffles –
a cold she had suffered all week –
and anyone's nose,
when it's blocked up
affects how they sound when they speak.

'That's it!' said the AA man brightly.
'Your words
must have sounded most weird.
Have a mint.'
And he gave her a strong one,
so her poor bunged-up nose
quickly cleared.

Then: 'LICKERTY-SPLIT!'
she was airborne,
shooting off with a wave and a grin.
She went supersonic to Blackpond,
coming down with a loop and a spin.

Meanwhile,
back at AA headquarters,
the young man was giving some hints.
'You don't need a toolbox
for broomsticks,' he said.
'Just a packet of very strong mints.'

Barry Buckingham

The River's Story

I remember when life was good.
I shilly-shallied across the meadows,
Tumbled down mountains,
I laughed and gurgled through the woods,
Stretched and yawned in a myriad of floods.
Insects, weightless as sunbeams,
Settled upon my skin to drink.
I wore lily-pads like medals.
Fish, lazy and battle-scarred,
Gossiped beneath them.
The damselflies were my ballerinas,
The pike my ambassadors.
Kingfishers, disguised as rainbows,
Were my secret agents.
It was a sweet time, a gone-time,
A time before factories grew,
Brick by greedy brick,
And left me cowering
In monstrous shadows.
Like drunken giants
They vomited their poisons into me.
Tonight, a scattering of vagrant bluebells,
Dwarfed by those same poisons,
Toll my ending.

Children, come and find me if you wish.
I am your inheritance.
Behind the derelict housing estates
You will discover my remnants.
Clogged with garbage and junk
To an open sewer I've shrunk.
I, who have flowed through history,
Who have seen hamlets become villages,
Villages become towns, towns become cities,
Am reduced to a trickle of filth
Beneath the still, burning stars.

Brian Patten

Late Home

I looked up – and the sun had gone
Though it was there a minute before,
And the light had grown terribly thin
And no one played by the shore
Of the lake, now empty, and still;
And I heard the park-keepers shout
As they cycled around the paths . . .
'Closing, closing . . . everyone out . . . '

Then I panicked and started to run,
Leaving all of the others behind
(I could hear their cries in the bushes –
It was me they were trying to find)
But they had the burn and the minnows,
The rope, the slide, the shrubbery track,
And the trees where a thrush was singing,
And I had the long road back –

The road that led, empty and straight
Down under the tall grey flats
Where the lights were on, and the tellies,
And old ladies were putting out cats –
I ran past them, without looking round
As if I'd committed a crime:
At six they'd said 'Just half an hour'
And *now* – oh, what was the time?

How could it have gone already?
Something must be, it *must* be, wrong –
I've only just come out – and why
Is getting back taking so long?
I can't be late – or if I am,
It's the fault of the sun or the moon.
When the dentist's takes an eternity
How are good things over so soon?

So I stopped and asked, 'Please, mister . . .'
And his left wrist came slowly round
And he peered at his watch, then shook it
Saying, 'Blast, it's never been wound.'
But the next man hauled his up,
Like a lead sinker on a line,
Clicked open the front, and boomed out,
'It's exactly five minutes to nine.'

– There's a great big gap in-between
The way things are, the way things seem,
And I dropped down it then, like you do
When you shoot back to life from a dream.
I stood there and muttered, 'It can't be –
His watch must be wrong' – then, aghast –
'This time, I'll *really* be for it.
If it isn't a whole two hours fast.'

But I got my legs going again
And ran, gulping in red-hot air,
Through backstreets where no one knew me,
Till I came out in the Town Square.
But when I looked at the shining face
And heard the cheerful chimes
Of the Town Hall clock – then every hope
Drained away, as it struck nine times.

Two hours late . . . two hours late –
Perhaps they've called the police
Two hours late . . . who, all in a line
Are combing the waste ground, piece by piece,
While *they* all stand in our window
Anxious and angry and, soon as I'm seen,
Ready to frown and shout, 'There he is.'
'Come here you!' and 'Where's the child been?'

– When I come round the corner and see them,
I'll limp, as though I'd a sprain,
And whimper, 'I didn't mean it' and
'I'll never ever go out, again . . .
How can I know that time's up,
When I'm enjoying myself such a lot?
I'm sorry – won't you take me back in?
Are you glad to see me, or not?'

. . . But later in bed, as I lay there
In the extraordinary light –
Filtering through the half-drawn curtain –
Of that silvery spellbound night,
I wondered just what *had* happened
To Time, for three hours in June:
If all of my life should be as happy –
Will it all be over as soon?

Brian Lee

Everything's Fine

First, we missed the turning off the motorway.
Don't ask me how!
I'd fallen asleep in the back.
I was woken by the shouting
As they tried to blame each other.
We had to drive another twelve miles
To the next junction
And another twelve miles back.
By that time it was dark.
It took us another half-hour
To find the campsite.
It's down this narrow lane.
Halfway along we met another car.
The driver just sat there,
So we had to reverse
All the way back to the main road.
By the time we got to reception,
It was closed.
It took us twenty minutes
To find the warden.
He kept complaining
That he was off duty.
Then, he couldn't find our booking-form.
'We're full up,' he said,
'Apart from the overflow field
And we're not really supposed to use that
At this time of year.'

You can tell why it's called
The overflow field.
The mud's inches thick
And it's right next to the toilet block.
I've left them putting the tent up.
I'm just phoning to let you know
We've arrived safely
And everything's fine.

John Foster

Death of a Ghost

Now none of us had ever
Actually seen the ghost,
Though some – like Raymond Pudsey
And his mate – would boast
They'd once stayed out all night
And seen it striding
At midnight past the ditch
Where they were hiding.
'Course, none of us believed
A word of it. *I* knew –
We *all* knew – Raymond Pudsey
Never spoke a true
Word in his life. But then
All of us believed the tales
Of the ghostly knight who
Roamed the hills and dales
Searching for the bitter foe
Who'd stabbed him one dark night
Nine hundred years ago.

They said the wounds from which
The knight had died
Still dripped fresh blood
That never, ever dried.
Many's the night I lay
In bed and couldn't sleep
Imagining I heard his footsteps
Climbing up the steep,
Rough pathway to our house.
My grandma'd threaten me
If I should misbehave with,
'Sure as sure one day
He'll rise up from the grave
And carry you away.'
'Don't you believe a word
She says,' my dad would say.
But even now sometimes
I wake up in the night
And think he's out there waiting,
Somewhere beyond the light.

Did anybody see it?
Colley's grandad did,
When rolling home one night
From Weston Dale so dead
With drink he slipped and fell
Into a field of corn –
This was long before
You or me was born.
He clambered to his feet again
And stumbled swearing
Through this sea of grain
The thorns and brambles tearing
At his clothes until
He staggered down the Fosse
Out on the moorland
Where the four lanes cross.
He stops. Hears a sound
And turning, sees this shadow
Rising from the ground.
'Course, first of all he thinks
What anyone would think:
Here's another bound for home
Something the worse for drink.
So Colley's grandad cries aloud,
'Who's there? Give me your aid!'
And not a word the stranger says
But three times waves a shimmering blade
Above his head, and striding past
Seems to vanish into air
Leaving the sound of battle
Still raging everywhere.

What was it like?
Its face was pale. It wore
A sort of chain mail hood
Which Colley's grandad swore
Was dyed deep red with rust
Or maybe it was blood.
Its eyes were closed,
The mouth a gaping wound
Screaming for revenge
But yet it made no sound.
As it passed it seemed
To do its best to strike
At Colley's grandad with
A kind of lance or pike.
And that was all.

Old Colley ran,
His feet scarce touched the ground
Until he shut the door
Behind him, safe and sound.
Shaking with fright, he fell
Into his bed and wept
With fear at what he'd seen
Till finally he slept.

The sun shone bright, the birds
Sang sweet the following day.
The apparition seemed
A million miles away.
Old Colley laughed and told his wife
What drink had made him see,
But she turned pale as gin
And pointed fearfully
To where her husband stood.

The white shirt that he wore
Ran red with crimson blood.
No matter how they tried
The blood flowed swift and fresh
Although no wound nor mark
Had scarred his flesh.

Well, that's our village legend
I've nothing more to say –
Except for something strange
That happened just the other day.
An Oxford archaeologist
Began to dig the ground
Where folk there reckoned
The knight would have likeliest be found.
For three long weeks he dug
While we all watched, our faces grim
Whispering to each other,
'What has *our* ghost to do with him?'

Then, one cold morning
Six feet beneath the ground
The man unearthed a coffin
And inside it found
Remains. The whole village
Stared in deep dismay
As our poor ghost was dragged into
The clear light of day;
A tiny pile of mouldering bones,
Broken wood and rust
And in the steady falling rain
A legend slowly turning into dust.

Gareth Owen

The Cupboard on the Landing

Mary had been told
Never to wipe her nose on her skirt,
Never to run in the house,
And
Never never to open the cupboard on the landing.

But one day,
After blowing her nose on a clean handkerchief,
She walked up the stairs,
Intent upon opening the cupboard on the landing.

First she
Turned the key in the lock,
Then she turned the other key in the other lock,
Slid back the top bolt,
The bottom bolt
And the six bolts in-between.
Then she cut through the chains,
Removed the barbed wire,
Switched off the alarm,
Threw her handkerchief over the video camera,
Undid the combination
And opened the cupboard door.

And what did Mary see
In the cupboard on the landing?
Nothing.
But
Something in the cupboard on the landing saw Mary.
And Mary was never seen again.

John Coldwell

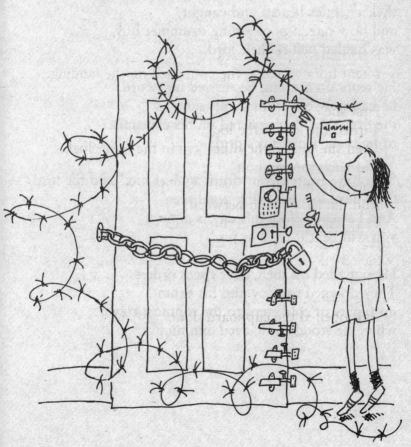

The Curse of Cortachy

Whenever the lords of Cortachy Castle
hear the sound of a drum,
their faces turn pale, they shiver
and fear the fate that's to come.

They remember a battle long ago,
their enemies beaten and caught,
and how one, a poor young drummer boy,
was hauled before their lord.

He wore no armour, he carried no sword,
he had only his drum by his side,
the drum that had spurred on his clansmen
to fight the Cortachy's pride.

'You have beaten your drum against me,' said the lord.
'You have lost me many good men.
And I swear before this day is done
you will beat it once again.'

He signalled his men, gave them orders.
They dragged the boy and his drum
up flights of cold steps to the topmost tower
where he stood, wide-eyed and numb.

They tied him tight and opened the drum,
they jammed the drummer boy in,
hoisted it up on the parapet
and spun it round on its rim.

In the one split second before he fell
the drummer boy screamed and swore:
'A curse on the lords of Cortachy!
A death for a death, ever more!'

Over and down went the spinning drum
and some said they heard it beat
a deathly tattoo, till it shattered –
there at the cruel lord's feet.

And now when a phantom drum is heard
around Cortachy's walls,
the family waits. Whose life will it take?
Who will die when the drummer boy calls?

Patricia Leighton

Cows on the Beach

Two cows,
fed up with grass, field, farmer,
barged through barbed wire
and found the beach.
Each mooed to each:
This is a better place to be,
a stretch of sand next to the sea,
this is the place for me.
And they stayed there all day,
strayed this way, that way,
over to rocks,
past discarded socks,
ignoring the few people they met
(it wasn't high season yet).
They dipped hooves in the sea,
got wet up to the knee,
they swallowed pebbles and sand,
found them a bit bland,
washed them down with sea water,
decided they really ought to
rest for an hour.
Both were sure
they'd never leave here.

Imagine, they'd lived so near
and never knew!
With a swapped moo
they sank into sleep,
woke to the yellow jeep
of the farmer
revving there,
feet from the incoming sea.
This is no place for cows to be,
he shouted, and slapped them
with seaweed, all the way home.

Matthew Sweeney

Danielle's Dragon

Danielle was sure
she'd seen dragon's breath
out beyond the headland.

'There's a cave in the next bay,' she said.
'That's where she'll have her lair.'

We said we'd go and look
but I knew before we set out
we'd be unlucky.

Just like our trip to the rainbow's end
or the afternoon we'd dug in the yard
thinking we'd reach Australia.

But Danielle was able to make us believe
we'd seen what she'd seen
and that what she said was gospel,
cross-your-heart talk.

So we trudged where the tide was out,
picking up this and that on the way,
till we rounded the headland and there
in the bay was some old tramp
with a bonfire, and smoke curling into the sky.

He was boiling something in a can
and he called 'Come on ladies,
there's plenty for all!'

But we took one look at
his gap-toothed grin, and his baked-bean cans
with the liquid in
and we turned and ran as fast as we could

as if dragon's breath was tagging our heels.

We couldn't have been more scared
if Danielle's dragon had really been real!

Brian Moses

The Election

The animals held a council
To elect themselves a king,
They wanted someone strong and bold,
Who could lead in everything,
The elephant was the council's choice,
Each member voted, 'Yea!'
That is, each member but the horse,
Who loudly shouted, 'Neigh!'

The vote had to be unanimous,
That's what they had agreed,
They knew without the horse's vote
Their plan would not succeed,
They thought it was important
To crown the elephant right away,
They had the throne, the robe, the orb,
And they had the horse's 'Neigh'.

The animals stared in disbelief,
Could there be some mistake?
They had to take the vote again,
And started with the snake
Who voted a resounding, 'Yess-ss-ss!'
The pig grunted, 'OK',
The little lemur said, 'Aye-aye!'
But again the horse said, 'Neigh!'

Once more they tried, and this time
The lion paced the floor,
He glared in anger at the horse
As he gave his positive roar,
The donkey gave his ass-ent
With a loud and lusty bray,
But when they all turned to the horse,
He hoarsely whispered, 'Neigh'.

'Don't you like the elephant?
Is he not strong and kind!
Is it his size that bothers you?
Is it his small behind?
Perhaps you want someone colourful,
D'you object because he's grey?
Would you like someone else?' they asked.
The horse happy bellowed, 'Neigh!'

The hyena laughed with crazy joy,
The others were exultant,
The cautious cat asked, 'Does this mean
You accept the elephant?'
Horse nodded fast and furiously,
They all shouted, 'Hooray!'
But when they came to vote again,
The horse's vote was – 'Neigh'.

They had to abandon the ballot then,
(According to the rule),
The elephant climbed down off the throne,
(A makeshift bamboo stool).
They cancelled the coronation feast,
As he watched them take the hay,
The horse hung his head in sorrow,
And sadly murmured, 'Neigh'.

So the animals went home kingless,
And (it's not widely known, of course),
The elephant, to this moment,
Is not fond of the horse.
Concerning that fiasco,
The horse would like to say,
He's not to blame, although he's tried,
He can't say aught but 'Neigh'.

(He'd like to say it, but of course, he can't.)

Valerie Bloom

Parentade

Once upon a time there was a small town
where all the parents got together to discuss
ways of improving their children.

See, the children were far from perfect.

They were often unkempt, untidy, ungrateful,
and a number of other words beginning with un.

They were often thoughtless, aimless, careless
and a number of other words ending in less –

and they were often disagreeable, disobedient,
    discourteous
and a number of other words beginning with dis.

The parents in the town were very worried about their
    children.
'The children of today,' they sighed with sad shakes of
    their heads,
'they're not like we were in our day.'

Then one of the parents, who happened to be a great
    scientist,
had a great idea – he could formulate a potion that
    would make
the townschildren perfect!

The great scientist asked the other parents what they
      thought of his idea
and when they all agreed that it was great the great
      scientist got to work.

The task wasn't easy but being a great scientist he soon
      perfected a potion.
He called it 'Parentade' and cunningly disguised it as cola
      so that the children would drink it willingly.
The great scientist just made sure that at zero hour
all the parents in town had enough 'Parentade' for each
      child in their household.
Then he sat back and awaited the results.
It was as simple as that.

What a transformation there was in that town!
The next day two hundred tidy children
set off to school in an orderly manner.

There they astonished their teachers
by being perfectly well-behaved and working hard.
At playtime the teachers couldn't believe how peaceful it
    was.
No fighting, no horseplay, no screaming – the school
    was perfectly quiet.

And so it went on.
At home the children tidied their rooms,
washed behind their ears,
cleaned the bath after use,
in fact did everything their parents asked!
From that day on all the children behaved perfectly
with never a murmur of rebellion.

But something was terribly wrong.

Perfect children need perfect parents and with each
    passing day
the parents seemed less and less perfect by comparison
    with their children.
The parents began to feel irritable, lazy, scruffy –
in truth they began to feel like perfect slobs!

The townspeople called an emergency meeting.
Perfect children, they decided, had been a perfectly
    idiotic idea
and they quickly resolved that the great scientist
should formulate an antidote to 'Parentade'.

The formula wasn't easy and the days that passed until
    he succeeded
those parents would rather forget. But at last, being a
    great scientist,
succeed he did.

At zero hour –
all the townschildren obediently drank the 'anti-
    Parentade'.
'Ughs' and *'Yuks'* echoed loudly around the town
as with much clutching of throats and rolling of eyeballs
the horrible transformations took place.

Very soon –
amidst sighs of relief and much rejoicing -
the parents saw that their offspring
had returned to being their former selves.

In the days that followed the parents were reassured by
the crooked school ties and uncombed hair,
by the increasingly untidy bedrooms,
by the whining voices of protest at bedtime
and by the dirt behind the ears –
that all was well again.

The parents were not perfect and once more neither
    were their children.
None of them was perfect.

They were all just perfectly normal.

Philip Waddell

A Tall Story

Yesterday Miss Williams told the class
'Use your imagination!
Everybody, close their eyes
(you too, Sophie).
Now what can you see?'

'Miss,' said Sophie, grinning,
'there's a baby alligator
lying on your desk.
He likes you, look,
his legs are waving in the air.
I think he wants his tummy tickled.'

'Well done, Sophie.
Excellent. Thank you. Everybody
open your eyes now.'
So we did.

And there he was, the alligator,
just like Sophie said,
and when Miss Williams
had tickled him enough she popped him
head-down in her handbag
with his scaly, waving
tail-tip sticking out.

'See you later, pet,'
she said,
'but, children, that's enough of that.
Pick up your pencils, now,
it's time to write . . .'

At breaktime, all of us
went up to Sophie
as she stood there, gobsmacked,
like a conjuror's assistant
who had managed her own trick.
'Sophie, you're brilliant,'
we told her.
'Wait till you hear *our* stories . . .'

Later, back home,
my mum, as usual, asked me
what I'd done today at school
and (when I told her) just for once
she didn't say, *'That Sophie!'* like she always did
but simply,

'You and your imagination!'

John Mole

Spinning a Good Yarn
– Read On

Young Oliver was born
in the workhouse
but
a passing earl
whose carriage wheel
came off just outside
the workhouse door
took a fancy
to his fair curls
and whisked Oliver off
to his stately home
where his wife at once
fell for Oliver's charms
as she held him in her arms.
So Oliver stayed
and grew up to be
a real little lord
(velvet jacket/own pony/toy sword).

Fortunately/unfortunately
the earl's eldest son
caught scarlet fever
and died so
Oliver, the adopted son,
became heir number one.
Whereupon
a letter arrived
proving beyond any doubt
that Oliver was
the earl's son after all,
the baby his wife had borne
in a swoonish fever
and quite forgot
(the earl being off
on the Continent).

Which just goes to show
I can write a Dickens
of a good story
with a happy beginning
and middle, as well as
a fantastic end
(and much shorter).
Over to you.

N.B. for *'fantastic'* read
'preposterous', *'unreal'*

Patricia Leighton

Not History, Her Story

George galloped along on his milk-white horse,
    feeling rather brave.
Till he heard a dragon's thundering voice
    from deep inside a cave.

'I'm not the heroic type,' said George,
    trotting away at top speed.
'I don't care what history says,
    Someone else can do the brave deed!'

Then he saw a lovely young girl
    tied with ropes to a tree.
'The dragon will eat me for dinner,' she wept.
    'Please help to set me free!'

'What me?' said George, with knocking knees,
    'But that dragon's a lethal weapon!'
'Lend me your sword,' the maiden said.
    'I can kill him myself, I reckon.'

So George gave the girl his shining sword –
    she freed herself with one stroke.
She thrust it deep in the dragon's insides
    and he died in a great puff of smoke.

'Bravo!' said George. 'The girl of my dreams!'
      I will make you my bride!'
'Not on your life!' said the maiden fair,
      'I have too much pride!'

She took the reins of the milk-white horse
      and sped off back to town.
'Tell it like it's supposed to be!' called George.
      'Please don't let me down.'

So the maiden told a fantastic tale, of how
      George had saved her life.
She helped him get into the history books,
      but no way would she be his wife!

Moira Andrew

Puss-in-footie-boots

The tale's been told many times before
Of Puss-in-Boots, so you know the score
But this one here is a brand-new story
True to form, Puss takes the glory

And this here is no fairy-tale cat
Or panto puss, she's where it's at
All flesh and fur, she's an actual fact
100% non-fiction cat
Now chill, relax, enjoy the match –
This brand new tale's about to hatch . . .

When Puss was a kit and no feet tall
Footie was her favourite thing of all
She wore her boots all night and day
And practised till she couldn't half play

Now once when she was down at the park
She heard a pack of hound dogs bark:
'We're one man short, so gave us a shout –
If you can help the Rovers out!'

So Puss stepped up, said, 'I'll have a game –
And you'll be really glad I came!'
But d'you know what? Those hound dogs howled:

A cat play footie? That ain't allowed!
As a cat can't kick – so a cat can't score
And a cat can't pass – with a little paddy paw
And a cat's too soft and a cat's too tame
So a cat can't play the big dog's game

Our heroine was not deterred,
With a Cheshire grin she softly purred:
'Boys, these sides aren't fair it seems –
I'll have to take on both your teams!'

They barked, 'We'll thrash you, pussy cat!'
'Oh yeah?' Puss laughed. 'We'll see about that!'

The whistle blew, the game began
And with that ball she ran and ran – till:
Goal number 1 – in one minute flat!
Goal number 2 – scored just like that!
Goal number 3 – a banana kick
Goal number 4 – a backward flick
For goals numbers 5 and 6
Puss used up more fancy tricks
She headed 7, own goal 8
So-who-do-we-appreciate?

These dogs went crazy, angry, mad
Whatever they tried, they just looked sad
They cheated, yelled, and made a fuss
But nothing worked against our Puss

Goal number 9 – a neat tail spin
Goal number 10 – just nudged it in
From 11 up to 21
Puss was having so much fun
The ref blew time at 24
Said ref: 'I can't watch any more!'

'Poor little pups!' Puss had to scoff
As she prepared to hurry off
And found her exit was now blocked
And then Puss had a bigger shock
Picked up, paraded 'round the grounds
And serenaded by the hounds:

She's fast she's fly she's sharp she's sweet
The niftiest feline on two feet
She's slick she's quick she's hot she's cool
And still she sticks to every rule
Watch her swing and watch her groove
You've never seen a cat like Puss here move!
Who cares if you don't bark but miaow?
We need you in our team right now!
And sorry 'bout us being so mean
but will you join the Rovers' team?

'Shucks' sighed Puss, and: 'Thanks for the game'
And was never seen 'round those parts again!

James Carter

Hansel

He was already two years old when I moved in:
grown to his full size, a big black backyard
    brawler
with the shredded ears of a veteran bruiser
but a plaintive high *Miaow*
like the cry of an abandoned child.

He wasn't very bright. In a rainstorm he'd ignore
the shelter of the apple tree, the warmth of the
    shed,
and sit instead in damp reproachful silence
in the middle of the lawn
till someone noticed him and let him in.

He disappeared when he was seven. A card in
the corner shop brought reports of a cat squashed
    flat
on the main road. We gave him up for dead.
He turned up six months later,
a little grubby, but in time for breakfast.

Every summer he culled the field mice that bred
behind the garden shed. And once I found
a disembowelled cock pheasant on the lawn.
Was it a fox's kill he'd found?
Or had the neighbourhood cats called a truce

and brought it down like dogs? Another mystery.
When the baby came, he coped. He learned
     never to
unsheathe his claws when ambushed in the
     garden,
or dragged from sanctuary
beneath the sofa by his tail.

She was often disappointed that he wouldn't play
like the fluffy kittens in her picture books,
but he was middle-aged by then, too old for
balls of yarn or cotton reels
tied to a piece of string; he had to

save his strength for new, more tiring, battles
     with the
ginger upstart just moved in next door. He seemed
invincible – until the abscess, then the flu.
All of a sudden he was old,
wanting to sleep all day on the piano-stool;

even the breeding mice, the fledgling sparrows
nesting in the eaves couldn't tempt him out of
    doors.
His appetite declined. Finally he gave up eating.
Sitting in the Waiting Room
I knew that he wasn't coming back.

He lay peacefully in the basket on my lap,
when once he would have screeched the place
    down,
clawing at the wicker to get out.
The vet took his temperature,
asked a few questions, sadly shook his head.

'What's best for him?' 'To put him to sleep
    tonight.'
As he spoke, the old cat crept into the basket
and lay down as though weary to the bone.
I stroked him one last time
behind the ears, and left him to rest.

Mick Gower

Haunted Dunwich (a true story)

The sea swallowed Dunwich. It gradually crumbled;
from cliff top to seashore it slithered and tumbled.
The sea swallowed houses, the shops and the churches
which fell to the beaches with shudders and lurches.
It gobbled the graveyards. The skeletons shattered
as down to the shingle they rattled and clattered.
Take a walk on the beach. Hear the screams of the gulls
and collect a few seashells, or possibly – skulls.
Explore the old village; it's all that remains
of the proud port of Dunwich. The small country lanes
lead only to cliff top. The treacherous sea
now covers the place where the town used to be.
But when sea mists descend (so the old people tell)
you may still hear a chime from a drowned Dunwich
bell.

Marian Swinger

The Weekend Camp

Friday morning and we started to arrive.
Our parents fussing, how would we survive
two days away from their loving care,
two days' adventure in clean country air
on one of our school's foremost annual events,
Mrs Blewitt, Mr Grice and Year Six in tents.

There was Jane's mum checking for facecloth and comb
while Sandra's fretted, they'd miss her at home.
There was Justin just bustin' to put one on Paul
(they've been like that ever since they were small!)
There was Michael with everything tidy and neat
and Nathan with Robin under everyone's feet.
Then Scott, all excited, jumped into the air
while his mum sorted out his underwear!
Sally chatted with Jane, 'What would it be like?'
while Linda swooned and swayed over Mike.
Then when all the bags towered high in the hall,
Mr Grice gave tail enders their very last call
and without too much more commotion or fuss,
children and luggage were crammed on the bus
where Gricey announced, 'Sit down and behave,'
till the bus rolled off and we all shared a wave.

The weather was cloudy with one or two showers
and the journey passed slowly, it seemed to take hours
till the bus bumped and bobbled into a lane
that was muddy and puddled from too much rain.
Then we shouted 'HOORAY' as we drew to a halt
and Gricey had a headache, said it was our fault!

When we got to the field the tents were all there
so we dived inside, then shot up for air.
'We'll have this place tidy in no time,' said Paul,
and everyone groaned, till we heard someone call:
'Hey you lot, quick, come and look at this . . . '
It was Michael giving Linda a sloppy wet kiss.
Justin had spotted them down by the stream
till Gricey came running and broke up the scene,
saying, 'Come on now, there's work to be done,
plenty to do, you're not here just for fun!
There's potatoes to peel and chips to be made,
beans to be cooked and tables to be laid.'

So eventually we finished our first outdoor meal
with the evening so still you could barely feel
a warm breath of wind as it tiptoed past
and Robin, as usual, was finished last.
So we dragged him up saying, 'Hey, let's go!
there's lots to explore,' but Gricey said, 'NO!'
He wanted six volunteers to wash up the plates
and he grabbed hold of me and five of my mates.
'Oh, come on, be fair, the girls will do it,'
but the look on the face of Mrs Blewitt
told us we'd better get on with it fast,
if this weekend camp was going to last.

Next morning, yawning, we were up with the sun,
and amazingly starting the day with a run,
but on the way back we met Garth and his crew
from St Barts C.P., and they picked up and threw
a number of missiles, though none of them scored
but we felt that this challenge couldn't be ignored.
It seemed they were camped in the field nearby
so we knew there'd be time to make our reply.

There was plenty to do, swimming or riding
at a nearby beach, rock-climbing or hiding
in smugglers' caves dark and deep in the cliff
but then Michael and Linda had such a tiff.
They wouldn't speak, their tempers flared
while everyone stood around and stared
until Michael mumbled, 'She's only a kid,
I couldn't care less,' but we knew that he did.
Then we heard him whisper to Justin who laughed,
'You know what I think, all girls are daft!'

But when we got back to the camp we found
everything trampled and scattered around
and a note that was pinned to a tent post announced
that Garth and his gang had called and pounced!

The note was red rag to a dozen angry bulls,
'We'll pulverize them, we'll abandon the rules.'
We pawed the ground and snorted out aloud,
we wouldn't be beat, we were far too proud,
Then Nathan declared, 'We'll get them for this,
we'll make them suffer, it will be bliss.'
But at that moment, who should show
but Gricey himself and he shouted, 'NO,
I'm not having any reprisal raids,
and on this subject I will be obeyed.'
So we mumbled, 'yes' underneath our breath
but we knew there'd be a fight to the death.

So we made our plans well into the night
and everyone agreed to a midnight fight.
All Year 6 would definitely be there,
including the girls who wanted their share
of revenge for the trampling down of their tent.
This attack would be such a surprise event.
We'd loosen their guy ropes and poles inside
so Garth and his mates couldn't run and hide.

It was dreadful that night, trying to keep awake,
Paul dropped off, but we gave him a shake
and Justin managed a kick or two
before Paul came round yelling, 'WATCH IT YOU'.
And Justin sneered, 'You and whose army?'
till we really thought that Paul would go barmy,
flailing fists and punching the air
while Mike said, 'Look here, you stupid pair,
can't you forget this silly pantomime,
save it for Garth, it's almost time
to meet the girls for our rendezvous.
Now does everyone know what they've got to do?'

The girls were waiting eagerly outside
so we made for the woods and a place to hide
while Robin ran over our battle plan.
But impatient as usual, Justin began
to strike out on his own so we had to follow,
across the stream and into the hollow
which brought us close to Garth and his camp
where we saw by the light of a single lamp,
eight tents that we'd have to deal with fast
if our element of surprise was to last.

Then we crouched there hidden by tree and bracken
while Paul showed us ropes that we'd need to slacken
so that tents would sway but not quite collapse,
before Jane gave the signal – three loud taps.
Then we crept up close, just as we ought,
four to a tent, but we all had one thought
would it work out the way it had been planned,
was everything clear, did we all understand?

And when the signal sounded at last
the tents went down, as Paul had forecast,
it caused uproar, such a hullabaloo
for there wasn't much any of them could do
while our side were sitting on heads and legs,
whacking backsides with thick tent pegs
until one or two surfaced, threatening and shouting
and we all took off as we'd finished our routing.
But they clobbered us quickly, fighting like mad,
it was really beginning to look quite bad.

The girls were all giving as good as they got,
Sal helping Jane in a really tight spot
while Justin was fighting alongside Paul,
and Michael with Linda was risking all
in a do or die confrontation –
Custer's troops v the Indian nation.
But just at that moment a whistle blew
and a teacher was shouting, 'That will do . . .
enough is enough, stop fighting, you hear!'
Then we heard Robin shout, 'Quick, disappear.'

All through the woods we heard bodies crashing,
yells and shouts and everyone splashing
back through the stream until safe in our tents
where we huddled round to discuss the events.
'We did it! We wopped them! We worked as a team.
It was really good. It went like a dream,
they won't have time to do anything back,'
and we talked and talked about the attack
while the sky outside was getting light
and we slept for what was left of the night.

Sunday morning, bright and clear,
'Not long before we're away from here,'
thinks Mr Grice as he heads for the showers,
looks at his watch, in a couple more hours
the bus will arrive to take us away,
then home at last for the rest of the day.
He scrubbed himself and risked a quick song,
nothing now that can surely go wrong.

Back at the camp there's no one about,
'We certainly must have tired them all out,'
he told Mrs Blewitt. 'It's been good,' she says,
'Yes, a really enjoyable couple of days,
nobody injured, we haven't had to shout,
no one in the stream, no one's fallen out.'
And there was Mr Grice smiling too,
good fortune had kept his motley crew
out of trouble, no need to worry any more
but he wasn't aware of what lay in store!

Then just at that moment a tent flap lifted,
somebody stirred, somebody shifted,
as one by one its four-man crew
revealed themselves, somewhat black and blue.
And from other tents, a similar sight,
as children emerged to blink in the light.
Black eyes, bloodied noses, arms and legs
scratched and cut, they looked like the dregs
of some beaten army, home from the wars
or cave men who tangled with dinosaurs!

Then slowly it dawned on poor Mr Grice
that despite all his well-intentioned advice,
no one had heeded a word he had said
and while he'd been sleeping soundly in bed
some terrible scuffle had taken place;
he lifted his hands and covered his face.
Mrs Blewitt found her girls were just as bad,
a shocking sight, 'You make me so mad!
You look like refugees from dreadful disasters,
come here, let me find some sticking plasters.'

Now Mr Grice was livid, we could all tell,
he'd turned sort of white and didn't look well.
'Don't you realize your actions were outrageous,
childish, immature, NOT courageous.
I thought you children were becoming respectable,
this sort of behaviour is just not acceptable.
On Monday I'll meet with our headmaster
and tell him of this weekend disaster,
and how Year 6 children are to blame
for ruining and spoiling our school's good name.
Now, everyone get moving, we've got to start packing,
not another word, and nobody slacking!'

Well the journey home was very subdued,
Gricey was in a terrible mood.
No singing or joking, he'd had quite enough,
he was feeling, he told us, particularly rough.
And even Justin, who always needled Paul,
sat very quietly, not bothered at all.
The bus behaved too, not a minute late
as we drew up alongside our school gate.
Our parents met us with sympathy and hugs.
We replied to questions with mumbles and shrugs.

Monday morning arrived, Mr Grice was still mad,
he felt let down, betrayed and quite sad
for he'd never had problems at camp before.
He gave two loud knocks on the headmaster's door.
'Come in, Mr Grice, do take a chair
this really is such an unfortunate affair.
I'll speak to the children, let them know they were
    wrong
to be quite so bubbly and somewhat headstrong.
In fact, Mr Grice, I find the story quite amazing,
our children retaliating, all guns blazing!
It must have been too much country air,
they'll write an apology and we'll end it there.'

Mr Grice wasn't happy, Mr Grice wasn't pleased,
he shot up from his seat and banged his knees.
'Headmaster, I must say, I'm dreadfully upset
is that all the punishment these children will get?
They were violent, unruly and the least I'd expect
is a little more support and a lot more respect.
Still if that's your decision and the end of the matter,
I won't waste your time with pointless chatter,
but if you're so keen on camping and the life outdoors
then next year, headmaster, Year 6 are all YOURS!'

Brian Moses and Ian Souter

A True Story

This morning on my way to school
just by the end of the muddy lane
where the bushes thicken
and the tree hangs down so it goes all dark
this man stepped out in front of me.

He wore a mask
with a ginger beard that looked stuck on
he had a stripy jumper, big black boots
a tall top hat and a swirly cape.

What do you want? I asked him
*I've spent my money at the shop
are you going to nick my sweets?*
He just grinned a nasty grin
and pulled out a massive sword.

It was a metre long and painted silver
he stuck it right under my nose
Right, he growled, *now listen here
don't muck me about, do as I say
I'm the Homework Thief
the dreaded Boss of the Homework Gang,
so hand over all your homework now!*

What? I cried, *You are joking*
I spent hours and hours on this homework
I did three sheets of sums and wrote a story
I got all. The full stops. In all. The right places
you can't pinch that!

Watch me, he said and snatched the lot
and then he'd gone, disappeared
into the hedge, which is why
I haven't got my homework, Miss
he's sold it by now to another boy
I'll do it again tonight, honest.

David Harmer

The Path to Lee

Some days are magic.

If I close my eyes
I see us walking across the cliffs to Lee
Under a shimmering sky.
I see the slope of the old man's garden
Where we stopped for tea and cake
While you chased the ducks
Until they chased you,
And a goat munched the bushes
Under a shower of purple butterflies.

I hear the rush of the sea
Where we caught a tiny, soft crab
In your bucket,
And because you loved it
We took it to lunch at the Café,
And fed it fragments of shrimp sandwich
Before we carried it home
To its own, dark pool.

Then the bus trundles me back, back,
Up the steep paths
Past farms and hedges of red flowers
To now,
To my quiet room
And my empty page.

But that day
Is still magic.
And it is only a thought away.

Clare Bevan

A Go'st Story!

Sir,
        It hath been a source of some regret
That thou should'st not have seen me yet.
Dost thou realize ye anguish and pain
Thou causeth me when thou hear'st not my chain
As it rattleth and scrapeth at stroke of midnight?
Gadzooks, man, it's meant to give thee a fright!
Thou always sleep soundly alone in thy bed
From whence, for centuries, all others hath fled.
I prideth myself on my dread apparition
But thou, alas, abjure superstition!
Now at ghostly reunions I'm made laughing stock
Because I'm unable to give thee a shock.
I've exhausteth ye usual haunted house tricks;
Sent icy draughts, snuff'd candlewicks,
Made ye door keys flyeth across ye floor,
But discourteous youth, thou continu'st to snore!
I'm sorely vexed, I've nothing left,
Of all good will I'm totally bereft.
I know'st ye fault lieth only with thee,
Researchers cam'st here from afar to hunt me,
So, I serv'st thee notice, tomorrow I quit.
My white sheet is pack'd for ye moonlight flit.
I go'st to a house where I knowst I shall merit –
For ye owners there know how to join in ye spirit!

Yours ethereally,
Ye Ghoste

Ray Mather

96

Girl Power

He was King of the Playground,
Lord of the Lunchbreak . . .
Always in the winning team,
Always first out, last back in
His voice was teacher-loud
His shouts bounced and echoed
Off the playground walls
His kicks fired the ball like a missile
Across the seething playground
And his tackles turned you over
With the force of a giant wave
All the small fry, the little fish,
Looked up at him with admiration
And a little fear

Then something happened,
One scorching summer lunchtime
With footballers all barechested
Like Brazilians on the beach
And girls flitting and floating
In butterfly-bright summer dresses
The King had hammered in a super goal
Hard, unstoppable . . . a winner all the way,
His small fans laughed and cheered
Ran to pat the wonderful back,
But one girl didn't, just his age
And just as tall, she tossed her ginger hair
Walked across the yard
And stood scowling right in front of him

YOU'VE HAD YOUR TIME . . .
YOUR FOOTBALL MATCH
ME AND THE GIRLS WANT TO DANCE
SO SHIFT OK
He breathed in hard, muttered something bad
And moved closer to the upstart girl
Then unflinching, she spoke in a voice
Just as loud as his . . .
I'VE TOLD YOU ONCE NOW SHIFT
ANY CLOSER AND YOU'LL GET
A GREAT BIG JUICY KISS
He turned away with angry eyes
And glowing cheeks, a group of girls
Exploded the quietness into cheers and jeers

On other lunchtimes
He still struts arrogantly around,
But we all know that something has changed
And the King seems a little smaller

Les Baynton

Index of first lines

Break out said the budgies, *bust out* barked the dogs   6

Cindy Reller   15

Danielle was sure   58

Dear Mr Pig, We notice   26

First, we missed the turning off the motorway.   44

Friday morning and we started to arrive.   81

George galloped along on his milk-white horse,   72

He was already two years old when I moved in: 77

He was King of the Playground,   97

High above the roofs of Paris   20

I looked up – and the sun had gone   40

I remember when life was good.   38

It was a Wednesday, I recall   28

I've had a horrible hundred years   10

King Alexander, third of Scotland,   8

Mary had been told   52

My dad was a kung fu fighter in a video game
    called Death Cult Army   24

Now none of us had ever   46

Old Peggotty Witch had a problem –   35

Once upon a time there was a small town   64

She was the Sleeping Beauty's   12

Sir,   96

Some days are magic.   94

The animals held a council   60

The sea swallowed Dunwich. It gradually crumbled;   80

The tale's been told many times before   74

They said they'd seen red squirrels, the people we
    passed on the way up.   18

This morning on my way to school   92
Two cows,   56
We went to Yalding to look at the locks   1
Whenever the lords of Cortachy Castle   54
Yesterday Miss Williams told the class   68
Young Oliver was born   70

Don't Get Your Knickers in a Twist!

Poems chosen by Paul Cookson

Don't Get Your Knickers in a Twist is a riotous collection of poems bursting at the seams with disorderly words, idioms, clichés and wordplay. You'd be daft as a brush to miss this side-splitting verbal jousting. Here's a little something to get the ball rolling . . . from 'Today, I Feel'

Today, I feel as:

Pleased as PUNCH,
Fit as a FIDDLE,
Keen as a KNIFE,
Hot as a GRIDDLE,
Bold as BRASS,
Bouncy as a BALL,
Keen as MUSTARD,
High as a WALL,
Bright as a BUTTON,
Light as a FEATHER,
Fresh as a DAISY,
Fragrant as HEATHER,
Chirpy as a CRICKET,
Sound as a BELL,
Sharp as a NEEDLE . . .

I'M SO HAPPY – I'M JUST LOST FOR WORDS.

Gervase Phinn

A selected list of titles available from Macmillan Publishers

The prices shown below are correct at the time of going to press. However, Macmillan Publishers reserve the right to show new retail prices on covers which may differ from those previously advertised.

A Nest Full of Stars	0 333 96051 3	£9.99
I Did Not Eat the Goldfish	0 330 39718 4	£4.99
The Fox on the Roundabout	0 330 48468 0	£4.99
The Very Best of Paul Cookson	0 330 48014 6	£3.99
The Very Best of David Harmer	0 330 48190 8	£3.99
The Very Best of Wes Magee	0 330 48192 4	£3.99
Don't Get Your Knickers in a Twist	0 330 39769 9	£3.99
Ye New Spell Book	0 330 39708 7	£3.99
The Colour of My Dreams	0 330 48020 0	£4.99
Are We Nearly There Yet?	0 330 39767 2	£3.99

All Macmillan titles can be ordered at your local bookshop or are available by post from:

Book Service by Post
PO Box 29, Douglas, Isle of Man IM99 1BQ

Credit cards accepted. For details:
Telephone: 01624 675137
Fax: 01624 670923
E-mail: bookshop@enterprise.net

Free postage and packing in the UK.
Overseas customers: add £1 per book (paperback)
and £3 per book (hardback).